The Day of the Black Blizzard

by **CANDICE RANSOM**

Illustrated by **LAURIE HARDEN**

On My Own

HISTORY

M Millbrook Press/Minneapolis

For my editors, Carol and Susan
—C.R.

To my father, R.L. Harden,
who instilled the work ethic in his children
—L.H.

The photograph on pages 46–47 appears courtesy of the Library of Congress.

Millbrook Press
A division of Lerner Publishing Group, Inc.
241 First Avenue North
Minneapolis, MN 55401 U.S.A.

Website address: www.lernerbooks.com

Library of Congress Cataloging-in-Publication Data

Ransom, Candice F., 1952–
    The day of the black blizzard / by Candice Ransom ; illustrations by Laurie Harden.
        p.   cm. — (On my own history)
    ISBN 978–0–8225–7895–6 (lib. bdg. : alk. paper)
    1. Dust storms—Great Plains—History—20th century—Juvenile literature. 2. Dust storms—Kansas—History—20th century—Juvenile literature. 3. Droughts—Great Plains—History—20th century—Juvenile literature. 4. Farmers—Great Plains—History—20th century—Juvenile literature. 5. Agriculture—Great Plains—History—20th century—Juvenile literature. 6. Great Plains—History—20th century—Juvenile literature. 7. Dust Bowl Era, 1931–1939—Juvenile literature. I. Harden, Laurie.
    II. Title.
    F595.R25 2009
    978'.032—dc22   2008026487

Manufactured in the United States of America
1 2 3 4 5 6 – DP – 14 13 12 11 10 09

Author's Note

The southern plains states are known as America's breadbasket. Flatland and few trees make it ideal to grow acres of wheat and other grains like corn. At first, farmers plowed the land and harvested their crops with the help of horses. During the 1920s, tractors replaced horse teams. Plows turned under prairie grasses and other plants that had always grown on the plains. Soon 100,000,000 acres of prairie became farmland.

In 1931, drought struck the southern plains. Months passed with no rain in western Kansas and parts of Texas and Oklahoma. Crops dried up in the fields. As the wind howled across the dry fields, the soil began to blow away. No one realized the native grasses had held the soil in place.

Dust storms swept tons of fine dirt across the sky. In the spring of 1935, these "black blizzards" battered farms for nearly two weeks.

Ten-year-old Orry Jenkins and his stepsister Mildred are not real. But they could have been any of the children who survived Black Sunday. It was the most terrifying storm during the long years of drought that lasted most of the 1930s.

Sunday, April 14, 1935
Southwestern Kansas
8:00 A.M.

Orry Jenkins took the cloth off his face.

He shook the dust from his blanket.

Black particles settled on the gritty floor.

Even though rags were stuffed

around the windows,

the dust always came in.

The 10-year-old slept

with a damp cloth on his face

to keep dust from getting in his nose.

Orry dressed and left his room.
Telltale boot prints down the hall
showed his stepfather
was already outside.
Orry's father had died years ago.
This past Christmas, Orry's mother
had married Dan Patterson.
They had moved to Mr. Patterson's farm.
Orry liked his stepfather,
but he wished he had a stepbrother
instead of a little stepsister.
Seven-year-old girls weren't much fun,
Orry thought as he went into the kitchen.

Mildred was eating breakfast,
drawing designs in the dust
on the table.
"Mornin', Orry," she said.
"What are we going to do today?"
"I don't know," he said.
With all the dust storms,
they'd had to stay indoors.

Orry's mother fixed him a bowl
of cornmeal mush.
Every day, they ate
cornmeal mush for breakfast,
corn bread and beans for dinner,
and corn bread in milk for supper.
Orry was tired of corn bread.
But times were hard.
Some families didn't even have that.

"The wind blew all night again,"
his mother sighed.
Orry thought she looked tired.
The wind didn't keep him awake,
but he hated the grit in his teeth.

Dust sifted into their food
and drinking water.
The heavy powder settled
on the chairs and tables.
It lay in heaps on the floor.

After he ate, Orry used a grain scoop
to shovel dust out the door.
Mildred brushed dust
from the cupboards.
Next, Orry wiped all the windows.
Outside, the sun shone
in a bright, blue sky.
It was a perfect day!
For weeks, the sun had been hidden
behind a cloud of dust.
"Can we go on a picnic?" asked Orry.
"We can if the car runs,"
his mother said.

Orry dashed outdoors.

His stepfather was in the barn,

working on their car.

"Will it start?" Orry asked.

Dan Patterson shook his head.

"Static electricity has nearly ruined

the starter," he said.

During dust storms,

particles rubbed together.

They created static electricity.

The electrically charged air fried corn

in the fields.

It damaged car engines.

His stepfather put down his wrench.

"Won't go today," he said.

Orry was disappointed.

He saw his mother dragging drapes
and rugs outside.

"Orry, come beat the rugs!" she called.

"Why can't Mildred do that?" he said.

"Because she's only seven,"
said his stepfather.

"And she's getting over dust pneumonia."

Mildred had been sick this past spring.

She couldn't cough the dust
from her lungs.

They'd had to rush her to the doctor
50 miles away.

"You're 10 now," said his stepfather.

"You have to be more responsible."

Orry was tired of doing most of the work,
even if he was the oldest.

After chores, Orry was free.
"Let's hunt for arrowheads,"
he said to Mildred.
Orry's mother gave him a chunk
of corn bread wrapped in a napkin.
"Don't go too far," she said.
Orry's dog, Archie, went with them.

They walked past barren fields
with a few straggly stalks of corn.
With the topsoil blown off,
the ground was brick hard.
How could anything grow?
Hot sun blazed overhead as Orry
and Mildred searched for arrowheads.

After a while,

Mildred said, "I'm tired.

Can we go home?"

"Not yet," said Orry.

Why did he have to be stuck

with such a babyish stepsister?

A stepbrother wouldn't want to go

back home so soon.

They wandered farther from the farm.

Once Orry stopped.

"Look at that!" he said.

Barbed wire was tangled

high in a tree.

Black feathers poked out

from the wire.

"A crow's nest," Orry said.

Even crows were having hard times.

They ate the corn bread
and rested awhile.
"I'm cold," said Mildred.
"Now can we go home?"
Orry was cold too.
The temperature was dropping fast.

Suddenly, thousands of twittering
birds fluttered overhead.
Archie started barking.
Why were the birds flying away?
Orry wondered.
Then he saw why.

23

4:00 P.M.

A black rolling cloud
filled the western sky.
Orry had seen "dust rollers" before,
but nothing like this.
The wall of blackness swallowed
the earth as it raced toward them.

Orry grabbed Mildred's hand.

"Run!" he cried.

The nearest house was too far to see.

Where could they go?

If only they weren't so far from home.

The sky was dark as night.

Dust stung their legs and faces.

Wind tore at their clothes.

Whirling dust blinded them.

Orry gave his handkerchief

to Mildred.

"Cover your mouth," he yelled.

What if she got sick again?

It would be his fault.

He saw a ditch next to a fence.

Orry jumped into the ditch,

pulling Mildred after him.

Archie hopped in too.

Static electricity danced along
the fence wires.
Frightened, Orry shielded Mildred
and Archie with his body.
Dust burned his nose like pepper.
The wind howled around them.
Mildred began to cry.

Orry was afraid they'd be buried

by the dirt.

"Stay here," he said.

"Keep your head down."

Then he crawled along the ditch.

He needed something to use

as a shelter.

The wind had blown all sorts
of things—boards, buckets, and
even a banjo.
They had gotten stuck in the ditch.
Orry's fingers met something smooth.
A sheet of cardboard!
He struggled to keep the wind
from ripping it out of his hands.
Then Orry felt confused.
Which way was back to Mildred?
Was he still in the ditch?
The world was all black wind
and stinging sand.
Don't panic, he told himself.
He was responsible for Mildred.
He had to get them out—alive.

Orry began crawling again.

The cardboard bumped his legs.

He stumbled over

a dust-covered lump.

"Mildred!" he cried,

shoveling dirt with his hands.

The lump stirred.

"Orry?"

Mildred was hugging Archie

and sobbing.

Orry held the cardboard

over their heads like a tent.

The wind tugged at it.

He gripped until his fingers ached.

The storm raged on and on.

They did not move from their shelter.

At last, the roaring stopped.
Orry pushed at the cardboard roof.
It wouldn't budge.
"Help me," he said.
He and Mildred pushed as hard
as they could.
The cardboard shifted enough
for Orry to stick his head out.

He gasped.

The world was covered

with black sand!

Drifts of sand buried the fence.

A strange orange glow

hung over the horizon.

Orry dug at the sand
until they were free.
Faces streaked black,
they walked along the fencerow.
Orry knew the fence would lead them
to a house or barn.

Sometimes the fence disappeared.

Orry scraped until he found the tops
of fence posts.

The orange light faded.

Night was falling.

Mildred stumbled wearily.

Even Archie had trouble.

Then Orry spotted a humped shape.

A house?

The dust-covered building
turned out to be a shed.

"We'll stay here tonight," he said.

"I'm cold and hungry," said Mildred.

There was nothing to eat in the shed.

And nothing to drink.

They were both very thirsty.

Orry thought Mildred would cry,
but she didn't.

He found some burlap sacks.

He put one around Mildred.

After a while, she fell asleep.

Coyotes yipped in the distance.

Orry was so tired.

He nodded off too.

"Orry! Mildred!"

It wasn't a dream.

A faraway voice was calling them!

Orry ran to the door,

but drifting sand had blocked it.

"Here!" Orry croaked.

"We're in here!"

His mouth was too dry.

He would never be heard!

"Can you yell?" he asked Mildred.

She tried.

But she could only whisper.

Then she picked up Archie.

"Speak, boy!" she whispered.

Archie barked loudly.

"That was smart!" Orry croaked.

Minutes later, they heard sand

being scraped from the door.

Then Dan Patterson burst inside.

"Are you okay?" he said.

"We're fine," said Orry.

"Orry made a roof to keep

the dirt out," said Mildred.

"And he found this shed."

"But Mildred got Archie to tell you

where we were," said Orry.

"You shouldn't have gone so far
from home," scolded his stepfather.
"I'll be more responsible
from now on," said Orry.
He had learned the power
of dust storms.
And he learned that Mildred
was no baby!

"Let's go home," said his stepfather.
"You two could use a bath!"
"And food!" said Mildred.
"I'm starving!"
Orry was starving too.
His mother's cornmeal mush
would taste great!

Afterword

The storm on Black Sunday ruined crops and killed livestock. Its winds raged at 50 miles per hour in a dust cloud 8,000 feet high. The next day, April 15, 1935, reporter Robert Geiger wrote a newspaper story about the storm. In it, he referred to the southern plains as the Dust Bowl. The name stuck.

Black Sunday spurred many farm families to leave. They came from Oklahoma, Texas, Arkansas, Nebraska, and Kansas. About 3,500,000 people packed their

This photograph shows a dust storm in Springfield, Colorado, in 1934.

belongings in cars and trucks and headed West. Many families moved to California, hoping to find a better life.

Despite hardships, most people stayed on their farms. Congress passed the Soil Conservation and Domestic Allotment Act in 1935. The government paid farmers to practice new plowing methods to keep the soil from blowing. They planted trees to prevent further erosion.

In the fall of 1939, the rains finally came. At last, the nine-year drought was over.

Bibliography

Allen, Frederick Lewis. *Since Yesterday: The 1930s in America, September 3, 1929—September 3, 1939*. New York: Harper & Row, 1939.

Bourke-White, Margaret. "Dust Changes America." *Nation*, May 22, 1935, 597–598.

Burg, David F. *The Great Depression: An Eyewitness History*. New York: Facts on File, 1996.

Ellis, Edward Robb. *A Nation in Torment: The Great American Depression 1929–1939*. New York: Capricorn Books, 1971.

Mitchell, Broadus. *Depression Decade: From New Era through New Deal, 1929–1941*, Vol. IX, *The Economic History of the United States*. New York: Harper & Row, 1947.

Riney-Kehrberg, Pamela, ed. *Waiting on the Bounty: The Dust Bowl Diary of Mary Knackstedt Dyck*. Iowa City: University of Iowa Press, 1999.

Stanley, Jerry. *Children of the Dust Bowl: The True Story of the School at Weedpatch Camp*. New York: Crown, 1992.

"Surviving the Dust Bowl." *The American Experience*. First broadcast 1998 by PBS. Produced and written by Chana Gazit. Coproduced and edited by David Steward.

Worster, Donald. *Dust Bowl: The Southern Plains in the 1930s*. New York: Oxford University Press, 1979.

Wunder, John R., Frances W. Kaye, and Vernon Carstensen, eds. *Americans View Their Dust Bowl Experience*. Niwot: University Press of Colorado, 1999.